AF587108

Art & Formatting by Shiane Salabie

Life's Purpose And Your Place

A Collection of Poetry

Written by Phil Ambrozy

This book is dedicated to my parents, Ann and Edward Ambrozy, for instilling in me a good set of moral values. I also dedicate this book to my loving wife, Janet, and my daughter, Miranda, for all the joy and love that they bring to my life.

Table of Contents

Reflection

Love

Animals

Life Experiences

Inspiration

Reflection

So Much To Be Thankful For

As human beings
We have a tendency
To desire much more than we own.
Rarely taking the time
To be thankful for
The precious gifts we've always known.

A romantic sunset
A picturesque mountainside
So many beautiful sights to see.
We admire the beauty of Nature
And we do it so readily.

But some people live in darkness
And cannot see the sky.
They cannot see the mountains
No matter how hard they try.

Have you ever raced through a pasture
And felt the wind upon your face?
Have you ever climbed a staircase
To reach a higher place?

Those who are unfortunate
Move about seated in their chairs.
Not able to run through pastures
Not able to climb the stairs.

Softly we listen to a bird's sweet song
Hear the laughter of children at play.
When someone we love
Says those "three magic words"
We are touched in a marvelous way.

But in a silent world
The songs and the laughter
Are too distant for people to hear.
Those kind, caring words
That warm the heart
Never seem to reach the ear.

A lovely home upon a lake
An elegant dinner for two
Living life in luxury
Is what we want to do.

But there are many people
Who sleep at night
With no roof overhead.
Others wander everywhere
Just hoping to be fed.

We often take for granted
All the things that we possess.
Frequently overlooking
The many people who have less.

So before you go to sleep tonight
And you dream about having more
Just remember how lucky you were today
There's so much to be thankful for.

Trust

Trust is just a single word
But it carries so much weight.
It means so much in a relationship.
It's what we look for in a mate.

It's the foundation a couple builds upon
As their love for each other grows.
When you have a partner that you can trust
You feel thankful for whom you chose.

There's a strong feeling of security
That you have with a trusting soul.
An honest and faithful partner
Can make a broken heart feel whole.

In a world filled with temptation,
Deceitfulness and greed,
Making a conscious effort to be sincere and kind
Is advice we all should heed.

There's not much left to a relationship
When trust succumbs to lies.
A love that used to flourish
Now quickly fades and dies.

It's possible to recapture
A trust that has been lost.
But anything highly valued
Will be regained at such a cost.

When we consider a lifetime partner
There are qualities that must exist.
Those that breed a trusting heart
Should be at the top of every list.

An honest and faithful person
Who is loyal and kind-hearted too,
Is someone worth believing in.
Someone you hold close to you.

Relationships have their ups and downs
Forcing people in them to adjust.
But the key to a loving and lasting one,
Is that single word called trust.

Destiny

There exists a mysterious force
That greatly influences the world we live in.
It dictates the paths our lives will take
And seems responsible for where we've been.

It appears that God controls this force
By waving His mighty hand.
The outcomes that result aren't meant
For us to understand.

Each life unfolds in a different direction
And what happens is meant to be.
The experiences gained along the way
Can be attributed to destiny.

It brings together lonely hearts
From places far away,
In an unexpected manner
On an unexpected day.

Although some of us are destined
To be successful and reach the top,
Others will suffer the hardships
That really make the spirits drop.

At times we feel that we're in control
Of the way things should happen and when.
But the feeling subsides when God intervenes,
And then we feel mortal again.

We try to predict the future
But there is no real crystal ball.
Each day that we live
Should be lived to the fullest,
Wherever the chips may fall.

Our lives take many twists and turns
That challenge us to the highest degree.
Our successes and failures seem all predetermined
By that force that we call destiny.

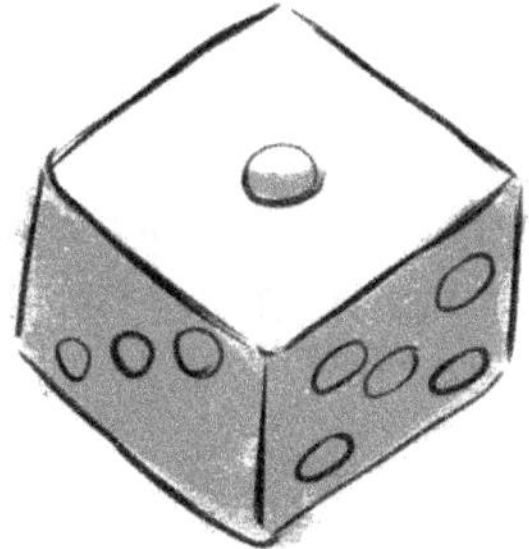

Have I Told You Lately...?

Have I told you lately
Just how much
I care for you inside?
How much I appreciate
Your love for me
And all the smiles you provide?

There are many days
Where I seem to feel
Like I'm always on the run.
Which makes it difficult for me to spend
Some time with my special one.

But I want you to know
That you're in my heart
No matter what's on my mind.
I love you because you're so good to me,
And because you are one of a kind.

Your companionship means so much to me
And your love means even more.
You're the reason why I'm happier now
Than I've ever been before.

The heart of gold that rests within you
Makes me thankful that you're mine.
When the good Lord gave out angel's wings
He put you first in line.

The Truly Good Things In One's Life

Each day that we wake up to
Creates a new page in our lives.
We can appreciate life's most beautiful things
And savor the many pleasures we derive.

A cool autumn breeze,
The smell of fresh cut grass,
And a beautiful clear blue sky.
These sights and smells and things we feel
Can really lift our spirits high.

The laughter of little children,
A dog's vigorously wagging tail.
These are precious moments
That make us smile without fail.

The vastness of the ocean,
The sound of waves crashing along the beach.
Late at night we sleep peacefully
Wondering how far our dreams may reach.

Looking beyond majestic mountain peaks,
Taking a dip in a natural spring.
It would be hard to find a sweeter sound
Than the song that the bluebird sings.

The warmth of an elderly person's smile,
The love of a caring wife.
These are just a few examples
Of the truly good things in one's life.

What Happens...?

What happens after you close your eyes
For the last time here on earth?
Is there a sudden revelation
About how much your life was worth?

There are people who believe
That when that final curtain drops
There's nothing left but darkness
And your thinking process stops.

But there are many people
Who have faith in God
That there's a better life ahead.
A life that's far more wonderful
Than any life they may have led.

It's filled with peace and happiness
There's no suffering or pain.
It's a life that's very positive
A life where you can't complain.

It’s a world that’s filled with beauty
And there’s harmony everywhere.
All the loved ones that you’ve ever known
Extend their arms to show they care.

The hopes and dreams you had on earth
Can be fully realized here.
If this is truly heaven
Then there’s nothing for you to fear.

When you close your eyes that final time
There’s a new pathway your soul will take.
One that leads to eternal happiness
As soon as you awake.

Thank You Lord

Thank you Lord for giving me
The breath of life each day.
Thank you for watching over me
While I'm at work and while I play.

Thank you Lord
For the healthy mind and body
That you have given me.
Thank you for all the wonderful sights
That you have let me see.

Thank you Lord for blessing me
With parents who really care.
Please thank them for all their sacrifices
And the many things they've shared.

Thank you Lord for my loving family
They give so much meaning to my life.
My brother and my sister,
A sweet child and caring wife.

Thank you Lord for the many gifts
That you have bestowed upon me.
Having food and clothes and shelter
Is in itself a luxury.

Thank you Lord for allowing me
To live my life the way I choose.
With your love and guiding light upon me
There's no way that I can lose.

Thank you Lord for a peaceful end
As I begin my life anew.
The greatest gift that I can give
Is to love and worship you.

Life

Life is like a jigsaw puzzle
With many pieces to behold.
Each new experience is a lesson learned
To conquer the many challenges that unfold.

Life itself is unpredictable
Especially when fate intervenes.
There are times when circumstances do occur
That tend to alter life's routines.

But there are many things you can personally do
To change the direction in your life.
The choices you make will determine
If your road will be harmonious
Or full of strife.

The lives of other people
Will influence yours to some degree,
But your life too
May play a role,
In someone else's destiny.

It's true that life isn't always fair
But it's still precious just the same.
Concentrate not on your disappointments in life,
But on the challenges you overcame.

Time is very precious too
For it is one thing you cannot borrow.
Make the most of your life
With each breath that you take.
You could be here today and gone tomorrow.

Fear

Fear is an emotion
That we experience from time to time.
It can be precipitated by the darkness
Or the perpetrator of a crime.

For some people,
Being at a certain height
Can be too much for them to bear.
Others get very anxious
When they travel through the air.

And then there are people who become afraid
When they feel like they're boxed in.
Still others, following a tragedy,
Are afraid to start again.

Fear can be quite evident
When you deal with the unknown.
There are people who have a terrible fear
Of ending up alone.

It can be a little frightening
To not feel confident inside.
When the fear you have
Comes from deep within you,
There's no place you can hide.

But there is someone you can rely on
When you're feeling insecure.
One who will give you the confidence
To find the proper cure.

I'll always be there to protect you
From anything that may cause you harm.
The safest place that you could possibly be
Is right here within my arms.

Your Future

Do you ever wonder about your future
And where your life might go?
Do you think one's future is something that's
Not meant for us to know?

There are many questions you could ask yourself
About what will happen to you.
Knowing the answers would certainly affect
The things you'd try to do.

How many years will you end up living?
Will you ever find true love?
Will the level of success you reach
Be moderate or above?

How healthy will your body be?
Where will you reside?
Will you ever meet that special someone
In whom you can confide?

Is it meant for you to raise a child?
What kind of parent will you be?
Will the final breath you take
Be filled with peace or jealousy?

So many questions to be answered
That only time will tell.
There's no room in your near future
For the past on which to dwell.

When you discuss life's many outcomes
There are two factors you must apply.
Fate and circumstances
Will dictate where your future lies.

Reflectors Of Emotion

When you look into a person's eyes
Do you realize what you see?
There's a feeling being expressed to you
And it's done so honestly.

Your eyes are like two mirrors
That reflect the way you feel.
Despite what you may say or do
Your eyes will show what's real.

Sometimes the face won't coincide
With the feeling that's within.
The many facades that people show
Make trust seem like a sin.

They come in several different colors
From dark brown to baby blue.
Your eyes reveal feelings
That say so much more
Than words could ever do.

From happiness and anger
To sadness, love, and fear.
Sometimes your eyes will accentuate each,
Simply by shedding a tear.

Your eyes are very expressive tools
That display all your feelings and notions.
Revealing to others the honest you,
They're reflectors of emotion.

Patience

Patience is a virtue
That is treasured by us all.
It allows us to keep our cool at times
When others climb the wall.

Good things come to those of us
Who have the ability to wait.
A slight delay is a small price to pay
For something that is great.

Mounting pressures and commitments,
Meeting deadlines on the run.
Impatience becomes evident
When our tasks do not get done.

Frequently we try to do
Much more than there's time in a day.
It's amazing how a deep breath can drive
Your feelings of tension away.

Setting up priorities
And keeping track of time,
Will help to avoid the waiting game
That we consider such a crime.

It's true that our time is precious
And things happen beyond our control.
Becoming a little more patient
Is a very attainable goal.

The Quiet One

The quiet one stays up late at night
With many thoughts upon his mind.
There are feelings within him
That he wants to express,
And words that he needs to find.

He prefers to express on paper
That which he cannot say.
Hoping to make a difference
In the lives of others,
In a very meaningful and rewarding way.

He writes about the kind of person
Each one of us hopes to meet.
A person with a heart of gold
Who will make our lives complete.

The quiet one is righteous.
His moral values are very high.
He believes that everyone can get along
If we put our minds to it and try.

He acknowledges the two needs we have
Of being loved and loving others.
He promotes kindness and consideration
Among our sisters and our brothers.

The quiet one doesn't speak very much
But he sends poetic messages
That we all comprehend.
Like being appreciative and placing high value
On an honest and caring friend.

The thoughts and the feelings
Expressed by his messages
Come straight from the quiet one's heart.
Hoping to bring people closer together
And keep them from drifting apart.

Angels Here On Earth

In your lifetime you'll interact
With over a thousand different souls.
Some will play major parts in your life
And some will have lesser roles.

And with each life experience that you undertake
You'll acquire a skill that will benefit you.
Being able to judge who is moral and good
And who to be wary of too.

But there are some individuals
Who shine with a light
That surely must come from above.
They possess unselfish hearts that are truly unique,
Full of compassion, kindness, and love.

Without a thought for themselves
They give unconditionally
All that they possibly can.
These kind-hearted souls receive their greatest pleasure,
From helping their fellow man.

Who are these people that fly high above us
And yet they have no wings?
They help us when we need them most.
When our final hope hangs by its strings.

These wonderful souls embraced by God
Have been blessed by Him since birth.
How fortunate we are to have shared our lives
With these loving angels here on earth.

A Materialistic World

We live in such a materialistic world
That we often lose our sight,
Of the things that we know are morally wrong
And the things that we know are right.

A kind and sincere partner
Who is considerate and faithful too,
Is worth more than all the riches
That could possibly be given to you.

An emotionally satisfying feeling
Is what you experience when you're in love.
It's a priceless feeling
That brings great joy.
The kind you have always dreamed of.

Great wealth, prestige, and power
May be the fruits of your success,
But you can relish all these luxuries
And still lack true happiness.

I'll bare my heart and soul to you
For I have nothing at all to hide.
Judge me not by what I own
But by what I have inside.

You can own the moon and stars
And all that glitters in the sky,
But remember the most precious things in life
Are those you cannot buy.

Nobody There But You

Do you ever stop and ask yourself:
"What kind of person was I today?"
"Did I treat my fellow man with kindness?"
"In a sincere and caring way?"

Putting yourself in someone else's shoes
Is an easy way to determine this.
If you think about how you'd like to be treated,
Then there's no way that you can miss.

Being kind and considerate to others
Is not a difficult thing to do.
The warm feeling that you generate,
Is a great reflection upon you.

But there are people who say and do things
With no regard for how others feel.
Sometimes the wounds that they inflict
Take years before they heal.

It's important to treat other people
The way that you want to be treated too.
'Cause you have to live with yourself
When you look in the mirror,
And there's nobody there but you.

Sad and Misty Eyes

There are times in our lives
When God will challenge us
By putting our emotions to the test.
Creating scenarios that cause us pain,
Or those that put our fears to rest.

He challenges our adaptability,
And questions our patience and emotional strength.
When it comes to achieving inner peace,
Are you willing to go that extra length?

Sometimes a golden opportunity is handed to us
And then it's quickly taken away.
Those individuals who achieve great success
Know there are dues that one must pay.

There are some people that God disables
Whom we cannot comprehend.
People who are in the prime of their lives
With so much energy to spend.

And when He takes away a loved one
The pain strikes very deep.
It's hard for us down here on earth
To accept eternal sleep.

When we wonder why these things do happen
May God hear our wailing cries.
It's at times like these that we'll look up at Him
With our sad and misty eyes.

The Beauty Of Mother Nature

The beauty of Mother Nature
Is evident everywhere.
From the bluest sky
To the greenest valley.
There's so much she has to share.

The sun rises in the east
And shines so brightly
Giving life to a brand new day.
The flowers become more beautiful.
The animals begin to play.

You can hear the wind as it echoes
Through canyons carved in stone.
You can admire the beauty of nature
With a friend or all alone.

A rainbow's pretty colors,
A mountain's majestic peak.
Take a look at the sky
And you might see,
A fiery comet streak.

The refreshing sight of a waterfall,
A bird's sweet serenade.
There are some boundaries set by Mother Nature
That man should not invade.

Preserving the natural beauty
Of this earth which is our home,
Should be a very important concern to us
No matter where we live or roam.

For Mother Nature took a great deal
Of time and care
To create all these natural treasures.
It's time now for man to protect what she's done
So that others may enjoy the same pleasures.

The Cries Of The Weeping Willow Tree

The cries of the weeping willow tree
Are soft but can be heard.
They sound like the wind
At the break of dawn,
Between chirps of the mockingbird.

Her branches are long and heavy.
They hang till they kiss the ground.
Listen closely and you will hear,
A faintly weeping sound.

Her feathered friends who fly overhead
Stop to rest their tired wings.
They sympathize with and understand
The sad song that the willow sings.

For years the squirrels have relied on her
To shelter them from the cold.
But their instinct tells them now to flee
And they do what they are told.

A light rain falls upon the willow
As it has done many times before.
The raindrops now become her tears,
As a distant motor roars.

A concrete jungle will take her place.
Has man no shame at all?
He seems content to sit and watch
The beauty of nature fall.

Extinction

It's been said that extinction means gone forever.
Wiped clean from the face of the earth.
Creatures that once were admired so greatly
Now eliminated for their monetary worth.

There may come a day when we will be unable
To watch the rhino roam the plain.
The eagle will no longer fly above us,
And man's heart will fill with pain.

The mighty whale would become a memory
And the world would be tiger-free.
The elephants would no longer flap their ears
And there'd be no manatees left to see.

It would be impossible to spot a leopard
If man killed each and every one.
One of nature's most beautiful creatures,
Silenced forever by a gun.

Invading natural habitats,
Polluting the water and the air.
Man's greed and selfish nature
Can damage wildlife beyond repair.

Every creature on earth has a right to exist
Living peacefully anyway that it can.
And whether or not it gets a chance to do that
Depends upon the compassion of man.

How Quickly We Forget

Remember me?
That friend of yours?
Who gave his heart to you?
I thought the feelings you had for me
Were the same that I had for you.

The laughs that we had together
And the beautiful moments we shared.
I thought we had love for each other
I know I really cared.

Your loving eyes and friendly smile
Your warm and passionate kiss.
It's no wonder why I feel inside
A certain emptiness.

The letter you got in the mail one day
Came from one who is no dancer.
Each day I searched the mailbox here
But from you there came no answer.

The phone that used to ring for me
I cannot hear at all.
Please pick it up
Just one more time,
And give me a friendly call.

You told me that I warmed your heart
Whenever I held you near.
Then why the distance between us now?
Were you not sincere?

I know your feelings for me have changed
But I'm still real glad we met.
It seems a shame that although you've gone
How quickly we forget.

Love

A Very Special Someone

There's a very special someone
Who feels I'm special too.
I love her deeply and honestly
And she happens to be you.

In a world that's vast and so diverse
God has blessed me every day.
I thank Him for watching over me
And for sending you my way.

You're a kind and sincere person
You're my partner and closest friend.
Please believe me when I tell you
That my love for you won't end.

When you look at me with those loving eyes
And you flash that friendly smile,
You make each breath of life I take
Seem all the more worthwhile.

You're beautiful on the outside
And your heart is made of gold.
You're the kind of woman any man
Would be honored to have and hold.

Sharing my happy feelings
And helping to ease my pain,
You always seem to remind me
That there's much in life to gain.

The little boy inside of me
Will sometimes show his face
And when I am unreasonable
You put me in my place.

Thank you for loving me
The way that I am
Despite my imperfections.
Your faith in me has enriched my life
In so many new directions.

I once had a dream
That I was kissed by an angel
And all of my wishes came true.
There's so much joy in my life
That it's easy to see,
That the wonderful angel was you.

The Most Precious Part Of Me

There's a very special part of me
That I want to give to you.
When you receive it you'll understand
Why I do the things I do.

Sending flowers to you unexpectedly,
Massaging away your aches and pains.
I'll always be there to comfort you
When skies darken and then it rains.

Sharing with you my innermost secrets,
Leaving love notes to make you smile.
The happiest day of my life will be
When we both walk down the aisle.

Fragile, warm, and full of love
Is this gift that I have for you.
It harbors all my deep emotions,
And keeps my body running too.

My greatest pleasure comes from pleasing you.
Pleasing you any way that I can.
Just knowing that you really care for me,
Makes me a very happy man.

You're the love of my life
The one I care for most.
How I treasure your company.
It's with great joy that I give my heart to you.
The most precious part of me.

The One Who Loves You

Have you ever felt as if your life
Was quickly passing by?
Only to have a special friend
Lift your spirits to the sky?

Did you ever lay beneath the stars
Feeling lost and all alone?
Just hoping for someone to cast a light
Where none had ever shown?

Have you ever met a person
That you loved with all your heart?
One who swept you off your feet,
Right from the very start?

There's a special person for each of us
Just waiting to be found.
A person who will return your love
And change your life around.

The smile upon your face
Reflects the happiness that you feel.
It's the joy of having met someone
Whose love for you is real.

So wrap your arms around that friend
Who means so much to you.
It's so wonderful to share your love
With one who loves you too.

Two Special Needs

Man is a very sensitive creature
With needs that are well defined.
To be loved by someone,
And to have love for another,
Are two needs that possess his mind.

An affectionate kiss
A gentle touch,
Is all that he requires
To make him feel that he's truly loved,
A feeling he strongly desires.

He searches for someone
To give from within,
All the love that his heart has to share.
His eyes seem to say
As he looks in your own,
"I love you, I need you, I care."

Love is a feeling
Man gives and receives
Sometimes it's too strong to be measured.
Sending warmth through the body
And peace through the mind
It's so wanted, welcomed, and treasured.

There are many feelings that man can express.
They range from pure joy to regret,
But nothing compares to the one that he feels
When those two special needs have been met.

A Love That Lasts A Lifetime

A love that lasts a lifetime
Is very precious and desirable.
It's expressed by someone
Who's sincere and kind,
And whose loyalty is undeniable.

The feeling comes from deep inside
And is shown in many ways.
It's the kind of love that's really true.
The kind that never strays.

Honesty and acceptance,
Mutual respect and understanding,
Two people can share an endless love
By being considerate and not demanding.

Patient and cooperative,
Affectionate and polite,
A person with all these gifts to offer
Is worth holding onto tight.

Expressing your feelings openly
And being gracious to the one you love,
Will help to solidify that special bond
People think so highly of.

It's hard to find a love that's genuine
In a world that moves so fast,
But what a blessing it is
To find someone
Whose love for you will last.

A Close Friend

A close friend is one
Who lies deep within your heart.
Always by your side
And never far apart.

He knows what's on your mind
And how you really feel.
He does his best to comfort you
And helps your wounds to heal.

A smile comes upon your face
With everything he shares.
It's the little things he does for you
That shows he really cares.

He shows love and affection
In a very special way
And when you're feeling down and out
He dries your tears away.

He came into your life
It seemed not long ago
But with each passing moment
You've watched each other grow.

The stream of love he has for you
Is one that has no end.
How thankful you must really be
To have so close a friend.

God And Family, Friends And Me

Do you ever stop to think about
Those who are close to you?
The ones that make each day of life
So bright and fresh and new?

Oh great God above,
I love you most,
For giving me a life to live.
Please guide me down the many roads
For I have much love to give.

My wonderful family,
They love me so
No matter what I do.
I wish I could do more for them
To show I love them too.

I cherish all the friends I've made.
Each and every one.
They care for me and share with me.
They make life so much fun.

The love that I have for myself
I place so logically.
When it comes to those I care for most,
It's God and family, friends and me.

When A Man Says I Love You

When a man says "I love you,"
Can you tell if he's for real?
How do you know if those tender words
Are really the way he feels?

It doesn't matter how handsome he is
Or how many riches he may possess.
Sincerity is not determined
By a man's level of success.

But if you look into his eyes
And feel the warmth he has inside.
The odds are pretty good
That he's got nothing there to hide.

If he brings you unexpected gifts
And goes out of his way to make you smile,
He may just be a man
That you'll want to hold onto for awhile.

If a romantic dinner and holding your hand
Are his two favorite things to do.
These are two more indications
About the way he feels for you.

He appreciates your positive traits
And accepts you the way you are.
Whenever you're apart from him,
He adores you from afar.

A man who truly loves you
Will want to give his heart to you.
At that point you should realize
That he's done all that he can do.

Receiving such a precious gift
Should make it crystal clear.
The love that he expressed to you
Was certainly sincere.

My Best Friend

It's not very often that you find someone
Who's the perfect fit for you.
Someone who has all the qualities you want
And makes your dreams of love come true.

Now I've been fortunate enough to meet someone
Who makes all the difference in my life.
A kind and caring person
Whom I'm proud to call my wife.

She's very loving and affectionate.
She's unselfish and honest too.
You get a warm and friendly feeling
When she turns and smiles at you.

A devoted parent, wife, and daughter.
She's a loyal and compassionate soul.
She can take a heart that's broken
And mend it back until it's whole.

The feelings she expresses
Are as genuine as they appear.
Nowhere will you find someone
More considerate and sincere.

My wife is a very special treasure.
I know she'll love me till the end.
I love my wife with all my heart.
She's my partner and my best friend.

A Mother's Love

A mother's love is a special blessing
That is always caring and sincere.
There's a strong feeling of security
Whenever mom is near.

She brought me into this complex world
And has been with me through every turn.
She taught me the difference
Between right and wrong.
A valuable lesson for me to learn.

Supportive and understanding
And never afraid to take a stand,
My mom has a very unselfish nature
And is always willing to lend her hand.

She's made a lot of sacrifices on my behalf,
And has furnished me with good advice.
She said that if I wanted people
To be nice to me,
That I'd have to treat them just as nice.

The love that a mother shows her child
Is the greatest gift that she can give.
Her love for me will be in her heart
For as long as she will live.

Two Lovebirds

Two lovebirds met many years ago
And a wonderful thing occurred.
They began to sing the sweetest song
That anyone had ever heard.

It was a song about love and kindness
That could warm the coldest heart.
When the two had sung the final word,
They vowed to never part.

Together they leaped over many hurdles
Some were great and some were small.
The love and respect they still show each other,
Gave them the strength to clear them all.

Caring and considerate,
In sickness and in health.
It was in each other's heart
That they both found their greatest wealth.

They raised three lovely children
And taught them right from wrong.
They taught them to be kind to others,
And keep their sense of family strong.

Today these lovebirds sing the same sweet song
That they sang many years ago.
Their love for each other has never diminished.
It still continues to delight and grow.

Animals

The Gentle Giant

The whale is a creature of enormous size
Yet he swims so gracefully.
He's a mountain that moves with a beating heart,
And is a magnificent sight to see.

Intelligent and able to communicate
He has a language all his own.
The whale deserves a greater respect for life
Than that which man has shown.

His songs echo throughout the ocean depths
His awesome strength can't be denied.
Despite his size he's gentle enough
To let a man swim by his side.

There are times when he will leap from the water
And land in a thundering splash.
Then he'll fill his mighty lungs with air
And off to the bottom he'll dash.

Man's greed is his only enemy.
His numbers dwindle every year.
If massacred to extinction,
His songs we'll no longer hear.

If he should disappear from us,
The good Lord will surely weep.
Let's hope the future will be a brighter one
For the gentle giant of the deep.

The Lopster

The Lopster wakes up every morning
As the sun begins to rise,
And like an alarm clock
He arouses me
With his loud incessant cries.

He doesn't stand very tall at all
But he's as cute as he can be.
He's lovable and lots of fun
And full of energy.

He'll walk with me in the morning
And then again at night,
With a curly tail
And a bandit's mask,
He's really quite a sight.

He's affectionate and playful,
He's sympathetic too,
And when you give your hand to him
He'll give his paw to you.

Always faithful and by my side
The Lopster is my best friend.
The love I have for that little guy
I know will never end.

Max And Jake

Max and Jake are two Shetland sheepdogs
That are as playful as can be.
Full of life and full of love
Each has a unique personality.

Although they aren't related
They're the very best of friends.
When they play together you'd be amazed
At how much energy each expends.

Now Jake has a bigger appetite
And Max is the older of the two.
Both of these pups were found it seems,
At a place called Bark Avenue.

Max is very easygoing.
He's obedient and very smart.
He'll lay his head upon your lap
And try to touch your heart.

Jake is very active
And likes to run around the place.
He's also warm and affectionate
And will gladly kiss your face.

Unconditional love and loyalty
Are the prime two messages these pups send.
That's why Max and Jake
Are two of man's most dearest friends.

One Smart Pup

It's not very often that you'll find a dog
Whose intelligence will stop you in your tracks.
One that would simply amaze you.
A loyal and loving dog named Max.

Now Max couldn't read the newspaper
But he sure knew how to spell.
He did everything he could
To win your heart
And he did it very well.

He loved to go to the park
Where he could run in between the trees.
Max was faithful and obedient.
All he wanted to do was please.

Now Max was a very attentive listener
And practically understood every word you said.
He'd recognize and comprehend
And then he'd tilt and turn his head.

Max is no longer with us now
But we can find him if we just look up.
You see God had a heavenly need to fill
And He filled it with one smart pup.

In Loving Memory of Max
2/13/99 – 6/14/02

The Night Owl

The night owl sits upon his perch
As the day turns into night.
The moon and the stars shine brightly above him
Creating a mystical sight.

He's nature's night security guard,
Observing all who sleep below.
Patient, disciplined, and very wise,
There is little he does not know.

He ponders life's uncertainties
And questions the things man does.
He foresees the world as it will be tomorrow
But still remembers the way it was.

Rational and perceptive,
Offering advice to those who ask.
The night owl has an answer
For every challenging and complex task.

His face shows no emotion
But his will is very strong.
Long ago he learned to tell
The difference between right and wrong.

In the dead of night a cricket chirps
And the wolves begin to howl.
No creature can escape the eyes
Of this ever watchful owl.

And when the sun begins to rise
And the darkness turns to light,
The night owl quickly disappears,
For he's a creature of the night.

The Perfect Family Pet

Claiming to have the perfect family pet
Is for many people
An easy claim to make.
But the most perfect family pet of all
Was a wonderful sheltie we named Jake.

He'd look at you
With warm and friendly eyes
And wait for an acknowledging smile.
Then he'd wag his tail in appreciation
Because that was just his style.

He walked around the block
With a feline friend
And played with a ferret or two.
It seemed like the more time
You spent with Jake
The more your love for him grew.

Intelligent and very quick to learn
He even knew how to spell.
When humans spoke
Jake would understand
Because he knew our language well.

Faithful and obedient
Loving and patient too.
Being able to please his family
Was all Jake wanted to do.

Jake always responded to your first command.
You never had to tell him twice.
If only children could obey like him.
Now that would be really nice.

Rest in peace my faithful friend.
We miss your loving and caring way.
What a joy it will be
For all of us
When we reunite one day.

In Loving Memory of Jake
10/20/00 – 8/19/10

Life Experiences

My Little Man

I remember the first time
I peered into the nursery
And saw my brand new baby boy.
The sight of him brought a tear to my eye
And my heart was filled with joy.

A precious new life
So innocent and small,
How quickly he seemed to grow.
The more I watched his personality develop
The more I loved him so.

A trip to the park
Meant a push on the swing
And a chocolate ice cream cone.
Each time my son
Showed his kindness toward others
I felt proud I could call him my own.

He loved to play catch
With his Dad in the yard
And he loved to be read to at night.
Special moments like these
Made our love for each other
Seem to grow to a much greater height.

My presence at school plays
And Little League games
I know meant a lot to my son.
I gave him encouragement
And showed my support,
The same way my father had done.

I helped him pick out
His very first car
And I calmed him before his first date.
He graduated from high school and college with honors
And found a job where he could educate.

Today my son is married
And has a family of his own.
The love and devotion he shows to them
Is the same that he was shown.

A special bond exists
Between a father and a son.
The traits we share together
Often makes us seem like one.

My son and I are still very close
And we get together whenever we can.
The good Lord blessed me with a wonderful gift,
When He sent me my "little man."

A Breath Of Fresh Air

I remember a time not long ago,
When my heart was filled with pain.
I could not feel the sun's warm rays.
All it seemed to do was rain.

I knew that deep inside of me
I had a lot of love to give,
But rejection sometimes makes you feel
Like you just don't want to live.

Life's too short to feel so sad.
What I needed to do was see,
That there was a lot of happiness to be found,
Right inside of me.

Time would slowly heal the wound
But a scar was left behind.
I wanted so much to share my life
With someone sweet and kind.

But then one night,
From out of the darkness,
There came a friendly smile.
A wonderful feeling enveloped me
That I hadn't felt in quite awhile.

She was attractive, warm, and full of life
With a style all her own.
By the end of the night it was obvious
That my feelings for her had grown.

The more time that we spent together,
The closer we became.
Neither of us wanted to play anymore,
The silly singles game.

I treasure the love that we have for each other
And the special chemistry the two of us share.
I can feel my heart beating with joy again.
She's truly a breath of fresh air.

My Father

My father is a very special man
With a heart made out of gold.
If you were to seek the ideal parent
My dad would fit the mold.

His kindness is immeasurable.
He's the most unselfish man alive.
If I were to become a parent
It would be like he that I would strive.

A loyal and faithful husband
An honest and caring soul.
His positive outlook on life
Is an integral part of the paternal role.

He pushed me on the swing when I was little
And taught me how to ride my bike.
As I got older I realized that
Our interests were a lot alike.

He took me to see my first big league game
And he showed me how to play ball.
He gave me encouragement when I doubted myself
And stressed the importance of giving my all.

He congratulated me on my graduation day
And again when I walked down the aisle.
If you were to meet him
You'd get the same treatment.
A warm handshake and a friendly smile.

A faithful supporter for the underdog
And always willing to lend a hand.
You can talk to my dad about anything
Because he's patient and will understand.

When I think about the kind of father I have
I feel very fortunate and very glad.
The world would be a much nicer place
If it had more people like my dad.

I Know Your Heart's Not Here

It's hard for me to smile today
Although I bet you don't know why.
I ponder questions in my solitude
As I gaze up toward the sky.

For you and I have shared a lot together
And at times we've drifted apart.
But even though you were far away
I kept your spirit in my heart.

It was hard for me to sleep at night
Knowing you were in someone else's arms.
You looked at him so lovingly
You were captivated by his charms.

I've spent so many hours
Wondering where we both went wrong.
And despite the many things that happened,
I felt it was together that we belonged.

Your smile and your laughter,
Your unique and crazy way.
These were reasons why I loved you
Reasons why I'd never stray.

I cannot make you feel for me
What you don't feel in your heart.
I believe the time has come for me
To make that fresh new start.

Only time will tell if the choice you made
Was the right one just for you.
I feel I have a lot to offer
To someone who will want me too.

Losing you to someone else
Was perhaps my greatest fear.
I just can't feel real close to you
When I know your heart's not here.

Somehow I Knew

Somehow I knew
From the first time we met,
That you were the one for me.
The one who would end my loneliness.
The one who would set me free.

Your pretty blue eyes
And your long dark hair
Attracted me from the start.
But it was the warmth of your smile
And your caring nature
That repaired my broken heart.

An aura of goodness surrounded you
That I noticed immediately.
I wanted so much to express my love
And hold you so tenderly.

We quickly became the best of friends
And made each other feel at ease.
Honest, kind, and considerate of me,
You always aimed to please.

For me, every moment we spend together
Is like a fantasy come true.
I'm the luckiest man alive today,
Because I fell in love with you.

A One-Way Street

For me, love seems like a one-way street.
It occurs quite frequently,
When the feelings I have for a pretty girl
Aren't the same that she has for me.

Her skin is soft and golden brown.
She gives off a special glow.
The kind you see when you meet someone
That you'd really like to know.

Her hair is colored reddish-brown
Her eyes a lovely blue.
If she knew how much I cared for her
I wonder what she'd do.

I'd love to take her places
Where she's never been before.
When I'm with her
I'd try to think
Of ways to please her more.

She does not hear the pounding
Of a heart that loves her so,
And when she seeks out someone else
The pain begins to grow.

I wish she would give me a chance
To show that I'm for real.
That everything I say to her
Is how I really feel.

I hope some day
I will find a street
With many intersections.
It just might be the one where love
Goes in both directions.

When The Sun Doesn't Shine

The sun rose up on a cold winter morning
And welcomed a brand new day.
The love I shared with my best friend
Was special in every way.

A loving hug and a tender kiss
Made her smile from ear to ear.
I always felt real good inside
Whenever she was near.

But then one day
The wind kicked up
And her love for me was gone.
The foundation we had built together
Would not be built upon.

A revelation of uncertainty
A heartbeat with a different sound.
My dream of love and happiness
Came crashing to the ground.

The sunshine that used to keep me warm
Now lies hidden behind a cloud.
The one I cared so much about
Has joined another crowd.

There are times when love can be so elusive.
It is felt and then it flees.
Leaving behind a broken heart
And cherished memories.

The night has come upon me
And there is darkness everywhere.
I yearn for her affection
But I know it's just not there.

Is it true that there's someone for everyone?
There's so much pain when a loved one resigns.
I wish she could look at me differently.
There's no joy when the sun doesn't shine.

A Spirit That Is Free

The wind blows briskly on an autumn day
Scattering leaves throughout the air.
The free spirit floats like a falling leaf
To a place that could be anywhere.

A world without restrictions
A world without routine.
The life of a free spirit is different from
The lives that you have seen.

So many things that she wants to do.
So many places she'd like to be.
Her indecisive feelings
Create an instability.

Unable to make a commitment.
Having flings that stop and start.
How painful it is to love someone
Who tears your heart apart.

She loves to be spontaneous.
She can be fun to be around.
But a free spirit has a difficult time
Keeping both feet on the ground.

I loved my free spirit with all my heart
In a deep and sincere way.
Those tender moments and loving touches
Are now lost to yesterday.

There's a lesson to be learned from all of this.
One that I now can see.
A broken heart is inevitable
When you love a spirit that is free.

There Will Be Times...

There will be times in all of our lives
When new challenges stand before us
And though we're content with the people we've met
We feel reluctant to leave
But know that we must.

And with each new challenge that we undertake
We bring with us a part of our past.
Cooperative friends and rewarding achievements
Are some of the memories
That seem destined to last.

When we close another chapter
In the book we call "Life"
We leave something special behind.
A personal influence that can lead everyone
To a key that seemed so hard to find.

So let us be thankful for the opportunity we've had
To enlighten each other and share.
The respect and admiration
That we'll keep for each other
Will be due to the fact that we care.

Inspiration

Wouldn't It Be Wonderful?

Wouldn't it be wonderful
If we all could live in peace?
And all the bloodshed man inflicts
Would permanently cease?

Wouldn't it be wonderful
If we could shake God's mighty hand?
And a feeling of togetherness
Would be felt in every land?

A society without labels
A world with equal rights.
Opportunities for everyone
With achievement in their sights.

A world that's free of poverty
There's no selfishness or greed.
A world where people lend their hearts
To those in dire need.

A happy coexistence
With God's creatures great and small.
Each allowed to multiply
And a tranquil life for all.

There's a deep concern for others
That's universal and sincere.
There's no such thing as loneliness
With so many friends so near.

It's the kind of world we dream about
A loving and caring one.
Where the darkest clouds seem to dissipate
And give way to a shining sun.

The Unique And Wonderful You

There's something special about each of us
That makes us so unique.
Maybe it's your personality
Maybe it's your physique.

Your individuality
Is yours and yours alone.
But life has many tendencies
To which each of us are prone.

The way you dress and carry yourself
The way you react to stress.
These are imprints of a style that you display
To a greater degree or less.

Your morals and your values
Form the foundation upon which you're built.
That's why some of us live with a clear conscience
And some of us live with guilt.

What sets you apart from everyone else
Are the things you say and do.
Take time out to appreciate yourself.
The unique and wonderful you.

It's Truly Great To Be Alive

Every morning when you open your eyes
Life begins anew.
There are so many things to contemplate.
So many things to do.

You can see the sun shine brightly
Against a blue and cloudless sky.
You can hear the chirping of the birds
As they go flying by.

Take a walk through the hills and valleys
Smell the freshness in the air.
Appreciate nature's beauty
That surrounds us everywhere.

Reach your hand out to your neighbor
And brighten someone's day.
There's so much pleasure that you can bring
By the things you do and say.

Life takes many unexpected turns
Bringing joy and sometimes sorrow.
And should your spirits fall today,
See the hope that lies tomorrow.

Feel the warmth of someone else's smile.
Tell a loved one how much you care.
Your wonderful qualities are treasured by
The ones with whom you share.

Life is man's most precious gift.
His strongest instinct is to survive.
Making a difference can be so rewarding.
It's truly great to be alive.

The Circus Clown

The circus clown hides his face
Behind a colorful mask.
Making people laugh at any age
Is a very rewarding task.

With frizzy red hair and a big round nose
The clown is a sight to see.
Running around with big floppy shoes
He's a master of comedy.

He'll make you laugh with a contorted face
Or maybe a slip and fall.
His zany antics and outrageous stunts
Make him a character you will recall.

He has no fear of embarrassment.
His only goal is to make you smile.
He'll take your mind off your anxieties,
And make you chuckle for a while.

The circus clown is everyone's friend.
He's a constant reminder to us all,
That we should fill our lives with lots of laughter,
And have ourselves a ball.

Every Time You Smile

Every day when I wake up
There are new challenges that I must face.
Meeting responsibilities,
And running from place to place.

At times my life is stressful.
It can be very lonely too.
But those feelings seem to disappear
When I stop and think of you.

Your compassion and generosity,
Your warm and friendly style.
Reflected in an instant
By your bright and shining smile.

You bring out the best in everyone
With your optimistic views.
It's amazing how a smile
Can quickly wipe away the blues.

You generate a lot of laughter
With your humor and devilish grin.
Laughter helps the heart stay young
When it comes from deep within.

Strangers quickly become your friends.
The attraction is very clear.
People get a good feeling inside
When you smile from ear to ear.

When it comes to helping others
You always walk that extra mile.
The kindness in your heart shines through
Every time you smile.

Giving

A giving heart is a wonderful treasure
That comes from God above.
Bringing joy and smiles to others
With sincere gifts of care and love.

A person with a giving heart
Puts others before himself.
Granting other people's desires
And putting his own upon a shelf.

Giving can be such an exciting thing
Sometimes more than words can say.
Like seeing a child's eyes light up
When he wakes on Christmas Day.

It's an act of true unselfishness,
An act of kindness too.
Giving is an act
That you are more than happy to do.

It's done without expectation
That you'll get something in return.
Giving is a lesson every parent should teach
And a lesson each child should learn.

It's not what you give that matters the most
But the fact that you really cared.
It's amazing how good you can make someone feel
With a little something that you've shared.

Brightening the lives of others
Should be an important part of living.
It's easily done with a kind-hearted gesture.
A gesture we call giving.

Every Time I Think Of You

It's not very often that you meet someone
Who has a dramatic impact upon your life.
A person you just can't live without.
A future husband or future wife.

That's why I'm so very thankful
That our paths happened to cross one day.
You're a quality person with a caring heart
And I love you in every way.

Your sincere and compassionate nature
Makes other people want to be close to you.
They notice how kind and generous you are
By the many unselfish things you do.

You brighten my day with your smile.
You give me hope when I'm feeling depressed.
Your inner strength and positive attitude
Make me feel like I've been blessed.

It would be very difficult
For me to live my life
Without you by my side
Because you warm my heart in a special way
With the love that you provide.

The wonderful qualities that you possess
Make you one of so very few.
I feel like I'm at my happiest
Every time I think of you.

You Just Never Know

Every day we live our lives
With a clock that ticks on down.
We question how much time we have
But the answer can't be found.

We interact with many souls
Who touch our lives in different ways.
Some for but a moment
And some for all our days.

Hold close to your heart those special people
Who mean so much to you.
Show them how deeply you appreciate them
For the wonderful things they say and do.

Tell a loved one how you really feel.
Never be afraid to be sincere.
Guilt is a terrible burden to carry
When your loved one is no longer here.

Forgive others for the mistakes they've made
For there are none among us without sin.
Share the joy of being alive with others
By opening your heart to let them in.

Never take your loved ones for granted.
Treat each moment of life like gold.
We really have no way of knowing
How the future will unfold.

Look a loved one in the eyes tonight
And really let your feelings show.
It's not wise to let another day go by
Because tomorrow you just never know.

Your Ideal Mate

If you could create your ideal mate
How would you like him to be?
Could you pick all the qualities
That you treasure the most
And love him unconditionally?

Each personality is so complex.
There are many traits from which to choose.
The “good” must always outweigh the “bad.”
Anything less and you’ll surely lose.

Some people like the “quiet type”
Who’s affectionate and always there.
Others prefer the “table dancer”
Who’s never afraid to take a dare.

Maybe your ideal partner
Has the same interests that you do.
Maybe his are different
And he can teach you something new.

But there are two things of importance
That you always need to know.
The way your partner treats you
And makes you feel,
Reflects the love he has to show.

Finding an ideal mate
Can be a difficult thing to do.
Keep your spirits up
As you search for him.
There’s someone out there just for you.

Hope

Life as we know it is so unpredictable.
It's like the ultimate roller coaster ride.
With times where we're filled with confidence
And times where we just want to hide.

We experience peaks of great jubilation
And valleys of deep despair.
Sometimes the circumstances that we face
Are much more than we can bear.

But through it all
There's a plan we can adopt
That will certainly help us cope.
It starts with a positive attitude
And having faith in a belief called hope.

Hope provides the strength we need
To overcome what we must face.
Guiding us through the troubled waters
To a warm and friendly place.

When the odds are stacked real high against you
And the path you seek cannot be found
Just put your faith in God and hope
And watch things turn around.

Now this turnaround may not be immediate
And a great deal of patience
May be required of you.
So keep your chin up and your spirits high
And allow God's hand to follow through.

It's true that life can be very difficult
And make you feel
Like you're at the end of your rope.
But even the darkest cloud has a silver lining
When you have faith in the power of hope.

Touch Me

Touch me in a way
That I have never felt before.
Fill my heart with lots of love
And make my spirits soar.

Touch my hand
So all the fears I have
Will quickly go away,
And allow me to feel that warmth again
To love another day.

Touch me and make the life I live
Feel even more worthwhile.
Touch my soul and I will gladly go
That extra special mile.

Touch my lips with your very own
So I may taste your sweet affection.
Please guide me and be my closest friend
If I lose my sense of direction.

Touch me with your eyes
So that I may see
A kind and sincere face.
Someone I know I can always trust
And whose heart lies in the right place.

Touch my mind
With the kind of challenge
That will bring out the best in me.
One that will allow me to show my strength
And help me grow intellectually.

There are many ways you can touch my life
And influence the way I feel,
But it's your love
That turns my world of dreams,
Into one that is very real.

Through The Eyes Of A Child

Children share an innocence
That is universal and sincere.
Their lives are shaped by the many things
That they see, they feel, and hear.

The adults they are close to have an influence,
Some to a greater degree.
The positive and negative experiences they have
Affect the type of person they'll be.

A kind word, a smile, a pat on the back
Do wonders for a child's self-esteem.
By building self-confidence a child will learn,
That disappointments aren't as bad as they seem.

Children have a need to be loved and supported
And should be encouraged to do their best.
When they feel genuinely cared for by others,
Their fear of abandonment gets put to rest.

Having good moral values and being honest and fair
Are valuable lessons for children to learn.
Compassion and kindness are traits that one shows,
But trust and respect must be earned.

Parents and teachers must set good examples
With the knowledge and experiences they've compiled.
Their actions and words have magnified meanings,
When seen through the eyes of a child.

My Very Best

When you set your mind upon a task
A decision must be made.
To make an all-out effort
Or to let that effort fade.

It makes no difference where you are
At work, at school, or play.
Every effort that you make
Should be the best you can display.

Success may not show up at first
But you improve with every try.
You can reach your true potential
By keeping expectations high.

There's a sense of pride
That you feel inside
For a task that you do well.
Each and every one of us
Has the ability to excel.

You can always expect a lot from me
No matter what the test.
I've got a strong desire to succeed,
And I'll give you my very best.

Another Year

Another year has come and gone
And all the books have been put away.
With the arrival of summer vacation
All the students are hard at play.

As a teacher, it's time to reflect
On all the hard work that you've done.
Shaping the adult lives of tomorrow
And being a good influence on everyone.

Some students have learned to read a book
While others have learned to share.
They're all better off than they were before
Because you took the time to care.

Your students possess more knowledge now
Than when they first walked in your class.
Some progressed real slowly,
And others caught on fast.

Some had come in tattered clothing
Others in designer jeans.
Some children's lives
Were touched by your smile
And some by another means.

Your hair may turn a little grayer
And they'll wear your patience thin.
But by showing children that you really care
They'll each believe that they can win.

The job a teacher does each day
Is an important one indeed.
Because before you see that beautiful flower,
You first must plant the seed.

A Purpose And A Place

Have you ever questioned your existence?
Wondered why you're even here?
Each of us has a role to play
But it isn't always clear.

By looking deep within yourself
You can find what's meant to be.
The special traits that you possess
Can change lives dramatically.

Become the leader of a charitable cause.
Be a ray of hope to those in despair.
Show kindness to the less fortunate
Let others know how much you care.

Adopt a homeless animal
Make an elderly person smile.
You can make a difference
When you go that extra mile.

For God didn't put you upon this earth
To sit and waste away.
Each of us must find that place
Where we can brighten someone's day.

When you take that final breath
What legacy will you leave behind?
Will anyone know that you were even here?
Will you be remembered as one of a kind?

Live every day like there's no tomorrow
And keep a smile upon your face.
Each and every one of us
Has a purpose and a place.

www.ingramcontent.com/pod-product-compliance
Lightning Source LLC
LaVergne TN
LVHW080205180826
845678LV00023BA/1750

* 9 7 9 8 7 9 5 4 3 7 8 4 2 *